13 Photos
Children Should Know

Brad Finger

PRESTEL

Munich · London · New York

Contents

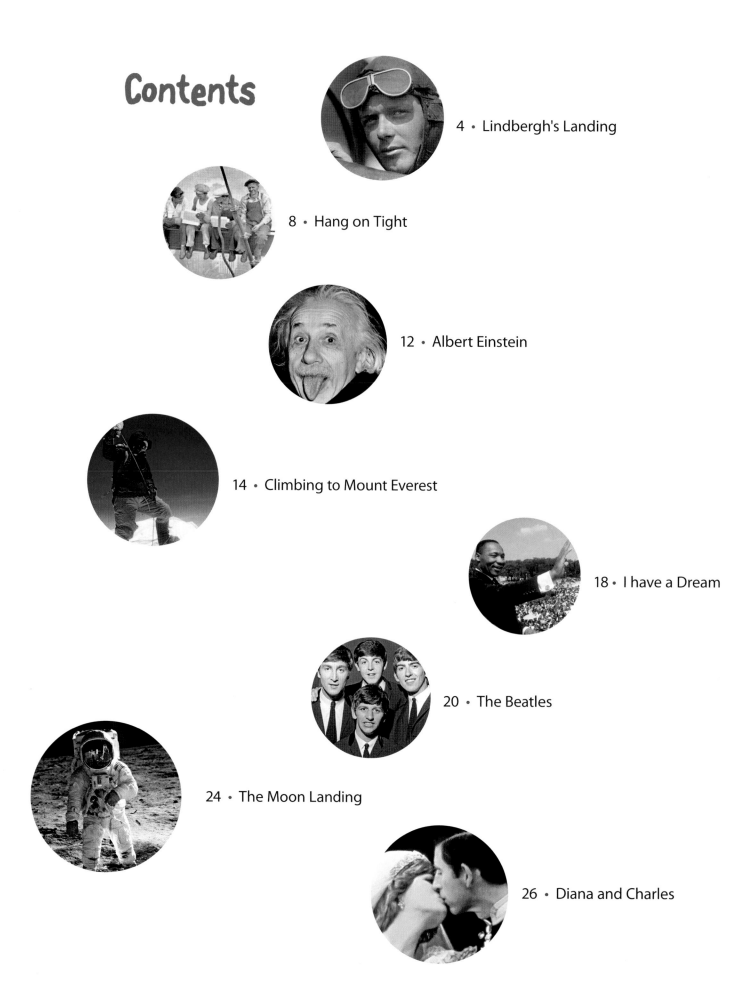

Magic Windows …

Photographs can let you peek into strange worlds. Some photos show you people who died long ago; people who dressed, worked, and lived very differently from the way we do today. Others take you to places you may never see yourself … places on the other side of the world or even in outer space! Still other photos capture important events in history, like a famous speech or a moment of discovery.

This book will show you thirteen photographs of some of the most important people, places, and events over the last 100 years. You will learn how these photos can reveal important things about the subjects they capture. An asterisk* follows some of the words in the book. These words may be hard to understand, and a glossary at the back of the book will explain them to you.

For each photograph, a timeline will show you what was happening in the world when that photo was taken. You will also find some quiz questions about the subjects in the book. If you want to learn more about a particular photograph, we provide tips for finding helpful books and places to visit. You can even learn how to capture secret images with your own camera … and with a little imagination!

Here you will find explanations of the technical terms!

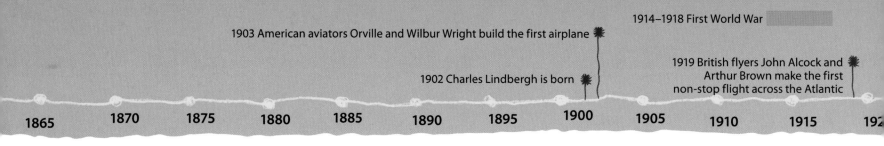

1914–1918 First World War

1903 American aviators Orville and Wilbur Wright build the first airplane 🌸

1919 British flyers John Alcock and 🌸
Arthur Brown make the first
non-stop flight across the Atlantic

1902 Charles Lindbergh is born 🌸

1865   1870   1875   1880   1885   1890   1895   1900   1905   1910   1915   192

Date:
May 21, 1927
Place:
Le Bourget airfield,
near Paris, France
Subject:
The Spirit of
St. Louis lands
in France after
crossing the
Atlantic Ocean

Tip
You can learn more about
Charles Lindbergh and
the history of human
flight at the Smithsonian
National Air and Space
Museum in Washington,
D.C. Lindy's famous plane,
the Spirit of St. Louis, can
also be seen there!

"Lucky Lindbergh"
Conquers the Atlantic ...

A skinny pilot becomes an American hero.

The date was May 21, 1927. Night had fallen at Le Bourget airfield, just outside of Paris, and huge crowds had gathered to see history being made. A young American pilot was about to complete a flight across the Atlantic Ocean, the first pilot to do so flying alone. His name was Charles Lindbergh.

Charles had survived more than 33 hours of dangerous flying—through bad weather and thick fog. Finally, at 10:21 PM, his plane touched the ground at Le Bourget. The joyous crowd mobbed "Lucky Lindy," and photographers were there to capture the thrill of that night in France.

One of the photos showed the crowd surrounding the plane, which was called the Spirit of St. Louis. Looking at this photograph, you can almost hear the cheers and feel the emotion in the air. Without such images, our memory of Lindbergh's achievement would be incomplete.

Charles soon learned that he had accomplished more than just crossing the Atlantic; he had also become an international celebrity. Few people— not even most movie stars—were photographed and filmed as often as Lindbergh. But Lucky Lindy's image represented more than just a famous person, it also became a symbol* of human courage.

4

1939–1945 Second World War

🌟 1931 Workers complete the Empire State Building, the tallest skyscraper in the world
🌟 1932 Amelia Earhart becomes the first woman   🌟 1950s Airlines begin using jet airplanes,*
   to fly solo across the Atlantic Ocean   making international air travel more common for ordinary people

1925   1930   1935   1940   1945   1950   1955   1960   1965   1970   1975   1980

Lindbergh lands near Paris, 1927

Charles Lindbergh wasn't alone when he completed his historic flight at Le Bourget airfield. Thousands of onlookers surrounded his plane, looking almost like they could crush it in their excitement! The crowd would soon carry Lindbergh on their shoulders in celebration.

Otto Lilienthal and his flying machine, 1894

Now here's a funny-looking creature … a human bird! Before the invention of the airplane in 1903, lots of people had ideas for how to get up in the air. One of the most famous early "flying" machines was made by German aviator* Otto Lilienthal.Lilienthal built his machine with a wood frame and covered it in fabric. Otto would use the machine to glide down a large hill near Berlin. Many modern hang gliders* are based on Lilienthal's ideas.

Amelia Earhart, 1937

Lindbergh wasn't the only American pilot who became world famous. Amelia Earhart, the first woman to fly solo across the Atlantic, was also a big celebrity. Many women even copied her hairstyle! But Amelia's life was not as lucky as Lindbergh's. She disappeared forever when her plane—the one shown here—got lost over the Pacific Ocean. Even today, people don't know exactly what happened to Amelia on her terrible last flight.

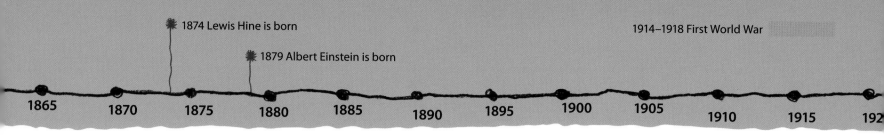

Photographer:
Lewis Hine
Subject:
Workers eating lunch during construction of the Rockefeller Center in New York City
Date:
1931
Place:
New York City, USA

Suggestion for further reading:
You can learn more about Lewis Hine's photographs of child labor in Prestel's *Lewis Hine: Children at Work,* by Vicki Goldberg

Builders in the Sky ...

An American city is remade.

Sometimes photographers have to risk their lives to get a good picture! Lewis Hine had spent his career photographing in places where most people didn't want to go. As a young man, Hine took pictures of ugly factories and run-down houses. He wanted to show how poor people lived in America, and his images shocked and upset many Americans. Some of Hine's most upsetting photographs pictured young children, often in dirty clothes, working in dangerous factories. These images helped convince the United States to pass laws forbidding children to work in such places.

But Hine's pictures were not all sad and gloomy. Hine was excited about the progress being made in American cities, and he photographed America as it rebuilt itself into a modern nation. Some of Hine's most exciting photos were taken during the Great Depression, a time when jobs were scarce and many people were poor. In the early 1930s, at the beginning of the Great Depression, Hine was asked to photograph the construction of two huge skyscrapers in New York City: the Empire State Building and the Rockefeller Center.

Hine could have simply photographed the buildings' construction workers from a safe place on the ground. But he wanted his pictures to show more than just men working. He wanted to portray how dangerous these men's jobs were … and how brave they were to do them. So Lewis followed the workers up to their precarious "office," the iron girders that stood hundreds of feet above the ground. There he captured them working, resting, and eating "up in the sky."

1939–1945 Second World War
1929–1941 The Great Depression
✷ 1931 Workers complete the Empire State Building, the tallest skyscraper in the world
✷ 1938 The U.S. government forbids most kinds of child labor

1925   1930   1935   1940   1945   1950   1955   1960   1965   1970   1975   1980

On the level, 1931

The Empire State Building was designed to be New York City's tallest skyscraper. So everything about the construction had to be done precisely. Here, Lewis Hine photographed one of the building's engineers* using a level. This instrument helped the engineers make sure that each part of the structure was in exactly the right position.

Hine's thrilling photos showed that ordinary people could still build great things, even during the Depression. They also gave hope to an America that needed to overcome hard times.

Eating lunch during construction of the Rockefeller Center, 1932

Anyone for lunch? Clearly, these workers were not afraid of heights. Lewis Hine's images show the courage that it took to build a tall skyscraper; courage that was on display even when the men were taking a break!

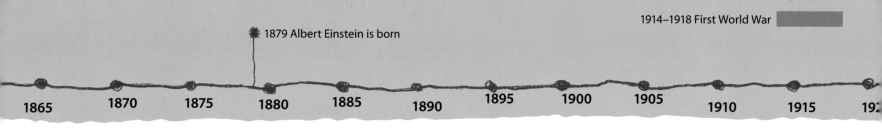
Portrait of Albert Einstein,
1951

Happy birthday, Albert!
Einstein may have been
a serious scientist, but he
knew how to be silly on
his birthday.

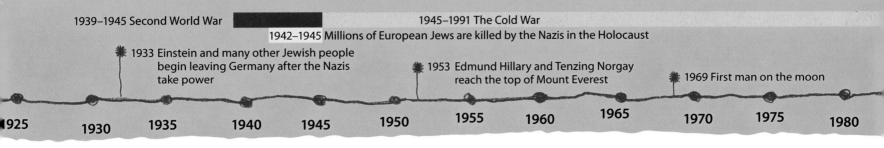

1939–1945 Second World War

1945–1991 The Cold War

1942–1945 Millions of European Jews are killed by the Nazis in the Holocaust

1933 Einstein and many other Jewish people begin leaving Germany after the Nazis take power

1953 Edmund Hillary and Tenzing Norgay reach the top of Mount Everest

1969 First man on the moon

925   1930   1935   1940   1945   1950   1955   1960   1965   1970   1975   1980

A funny Genius ...

Albert Einstein shows his loose tongue.

Photographs often portray important people in unexpected ways. In 1951, most people considered Albert Einstein to be the most brilliant scientist in the world. His ideas were used to develop the atomic bomb,* and they would soon help people learn how to travel in outer space.

But Albert was also a man who liked jokes and having fun. This side of Einstein comes through in Arthur Sasse's famous portrait photograph. Sasse took Einstein's photo at the Institute for Advanced Study in Princeton. Einstein was celebrating his birthday; and when Sasse asked him to smile for a picture, he stuck his tongue out instead!

Albert immediately liked this silly portrait. He also may have found a deeper meaning in the photo. Einstein sent copies of the picture to a news reporter, and he included a message that read "This gesture you will like, because it is aimed at all of humanity." Einstein disapproved of McCarthyism,* a belief that some United States leaders held at that time. These leaders thought that many Americans were disloyal to the United States and supported the Communist* Soviet Union, America's chief rival. So the government began accusing scientists, writers, and other important people of being Communists. Many of these people lost their jobs.

Einstein believed that McCarthyism harmed innocent people. He may also have wanted to show his disapproval of McCarthyism in a funny way … by showing his tongue to the world!

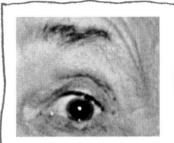

Photographer:
Arthur Sasse
Subject:
Portrait of
Albert Einstein on
his 72nd birthday
Date:
March 14, 1951
Place:
Princeton,
New Jersey, USA

Good to know:
Albert Einstein was not
only a great scientist; he
could also play the violin!

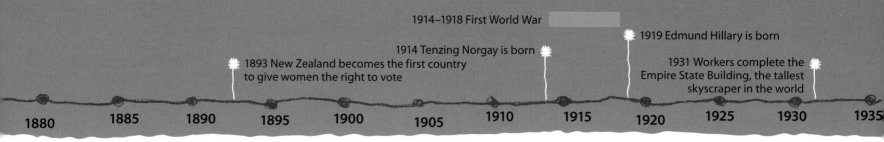

1914–1918 First World War

1914 Tenzing Norgay is born

1893 New Zealand becomes the first country
to give women the right to vote

1919 Edmund Hillary is born

1931 Workers complete the
Empire State Building, the tallest
skyscraper in the world

1880   1885   1890   1895   1900   1905   1910   1915   1920   1925   1930   1935

Photographer:
Edmund Hillary
Subject:
Tenzing Norgay
stands on Everest´s
summit
Date:
May 29, 1953
Place:
Mount Everest,
Nepal

Good to know:
After climbing Mount
Everest, Edmund Hillary
never stopped exploring
new places. He would
travel to both ends of the
Earth: the south pole and
the north pole!

At the Top of the World ...

Edmund Hillary and Tenzing Norgay climb
a mighty mountain.

The top of Mount Everest is the highest place on Earth … and one of
the most dangerous. No plants or animals live there. People who have
tried to climb Everest have often died. The route up the mountain is
treacherous, full of steep slopes and thick snow. And because the peak
is so high up, the air is thin and hard to breath. Before 1953, Everest had
not been conquered by any known person. Then Edmund Hillary and
Tenzing Norgay came along.

Edmund Hillary was from New Zealand; a long way from the Asian nation
of Nepal, where the top of Everest stands. Edmund began climbing
mountains as a teenager, and he reached his country's highest peak—
Mount Cook—in 1948. But these feats weren't enough for him. Edmund
wanted to reach the top of the world.

Then in 1953, he began preparing to accomplish his dream. Hillary knew
he couldn't make the climb alone, so he befriended a Nepalese man
named Tenzing Norgay. Tenzing belonged to a group of people called
the Sherpa, who live high up in the Himalaya* and know a lot about
climbing mountains. Edmund believed Tenzing's knowledge would be
important if the two were to make it all the way to Mount Everest's peak.

14

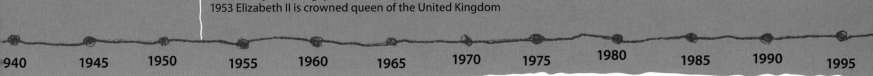
In March of 1953, Edmund and Tenzing began their journey with a large group of British and Sherpa explorers. All the climbers started together, but eventually Hillary and Tenzing split off from the rest … following their own route to the top. Using ropes and ice axes,* they slowly made their way up the icy cliffs. As they climbed higher, the weather became bitterly cold, but the two explorers didn't give up. They finally reached the top on May 29.

Overjoyed, Edmund took out his camera and snapped a picture of Tenzing at the summit. This photo became one of the most famous in the history of exploration. For the first time, people around the world could get a glimpse of the highest place on Earth!

Tenzing Norgay on the top of Mt. Everest, 1953

Tenzing Norgay holds an ice axe with many flags. He and Hillary knew that their achievement would be celebrated by people around the world.

Edmund Hillary and Tenzing Norgay on the southeast ridge of Mt. Everest, 1953

We're on our way! Hillary and Norgay had their picture taken just before they set out to conquer Mt. Everest's highest peak. The jagged cliffs of the Himalaya spread out behind them; a treacherous land of wind, snow, and ice.

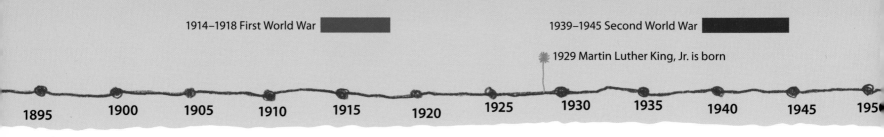

Photographer:
Francis Miller
Subject:
Martin Luther King, Jr. waves to thousands at the "March on Washington"
Date:
August 28, 1963
Place:
The Lincoln Memorial in Washington, D.C., USA

Tip:
The Martin Luther King, Jr. National Historic Site in Atlanta, USA will teach you more about this civil rights leader. You can visit the home where Martin was born … and see photographs of the most famous moments in King's life.

A Leader and a Dream …

The power of words and images to change society.

Reverend Martin Luther King, Jr. was a Christian preacher, and he loved to communicate with words. He used words to convince his churchgoers to treat others kindly and fairly—just as the Christian Bible commands. King also used words to achieve different goals. In Martin's day, he and other African-Americans didn't have the same opportunities as white Americans. Laws kept black Americans from attending the best public schools or getting the best jobs. Many blacks couldn't stay in white-run hotels, eat in white-owned businesses, or even drink from white-only drinking fountains!

Martin knew these inequalities were wrong and had to be ended. So he began convincing American leaders to change the laws that hurt African Americans. King and his friends led long walks in the southern United States, where some of the most racist* laws still existed. King also made famous speeches promoting civil rights* for all Americans, not just whites.

Then in 1963, Martin traveled to Washington, D.C. to make his most famous speech. Thousands of people heard King speak in person that day, and millions more saw him on television. Martin told the crowd that he had "a dream" that one day, everyone in America would be treated equally and could live together happily. Images of King addressing the huge crowd … a crowd made up of white and black Americans standing side–by–side … helped convince most viewers that Martin's words were true.

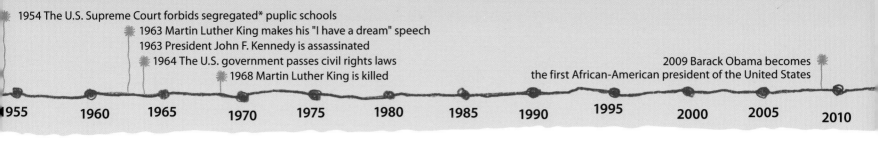

1954 The U.S. Supreme Court forbids segregated* puplic schools
1963 Martin Luther King makes his "I have a dream" speech
1963 President John F. Kennedy is assassinated
1964 The U.S. government passes civil rights laws
1968 Martin Luther King is killed

2009 Barack Obama becomes
the first African-American president of the United States

1955   1960   1965   1970   1975   1980   1985   1990   1995   2000   2005   2010

In 1964, the United States government would pass laws that gave civil rights to all Americans. But Martin's dream of a peaceful America would not come true right away. King would be killed by an assassin* in 1968. Yet his words and image still live with Americans today.

Martin Luther King speaks to America, 1963

Martin Luther King wanted black and white Americans to live together as equals. When he made his "I have a dream" speech in Washington D.C. in 1963, photos showed black and white listeners standing together in peace to listen to him.

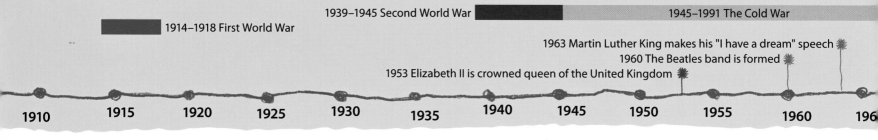

1939–1945 Second World War   1945–1991 The Cold War

1914–1918 First World War

1963 Martin Luther King makes his "I have a dream" speech

1960 The Beatles band is formed

1953 Elizabeth II is crowned queen of the United Kingdom

1910   1915   1920   1925   1930   1935   1940   1945   1950   1955   1960   196

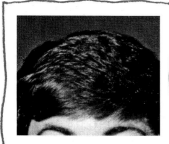

Photographer:
David Farrell
Subject:
The Beatles pose
for a group portrait
Date:
1963
Place:
London,
United Kingdom

Photography of Fame ...

The Beatles pose for for the camera.

Introducing …. the Beatles! The year 1963 was a big one for John Lennon, Paul McCartney, George Harrison, and Ringo Starr. The rock stars from Liverpool, England had just released their hit record, "Please, please me," and fans couldn't get enough of them. Soon, they would travel to the United States and become the most famous band in rock history.

The Beatles could excite people like no other band before them … or since. Huge crowds of fans, many of them women, would fill their concerts; screaming and shouting in delight as they played. Beatles concerts would become so noisy that the band members could barely hear themselves play!

But in 1963, John, Paul, George, and Ringo were still at the beginning of their careers. This publicity photo* shows the four young men the way they wanted to be seen. They look relaxed and confident, ready to play their music for the world … and ready to have some fun as well. They also show off their famous mop-top* haircuts, which were new in 1963. Before the Beatles, most young men wore their hair very short. But photographs like this one helped change all that. Soon everyone began growing their hair longer and longer.

Today, celebrity photographs continue to affect the way we dress, cut our hair, listen to music, and watch movies. Have you ever wanted to dress or look like a favorite movie star or musician? Chances are you have been influenced by photographs, just like the fans of the Beatles were!

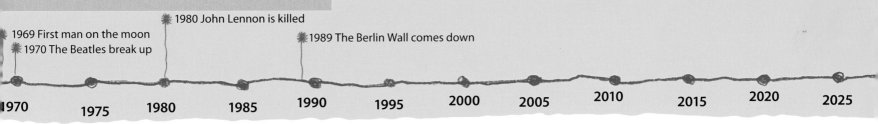

The Beatles, 1963

Everyone wanted to take the Beatles' portrait in the 1960s. What band do you like best?

Try to make your own fancy portrait photo. You and a friend can dress up like your favorite singer or movie star ... or just wear the clothes you like best. Then the two of you can take each other's celebrity photograph. Be sure to pose for the camera!

Beatles fans outside Buckingham Palace, London, 1965

Beatlemania hits London! Wild fans try to push past police as the Beatles arrive at Buckingham Palace to meet Queen Elizabeth II. Photographs like this one show the kind of excitement that surrounded John, Paul, George, and Ringo.

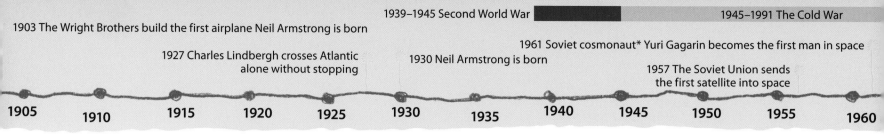

1939–1945 Second World War   1945–1991 The Cold War

1903 The Wright Brothers build the first airplane Neil Armstrong is born

1927 Charles Lindbergh crosses Atlantic
alone without stopping

1961 Soviet cosmonaut* Yuri Gagarin becomes the first man in space

1930 Neil Armstrong is born

1957 The Soviet Union sends
the first satellite into space

1905   1910   1915   1920   1925   1930   1935   1940   1945   1950   1955   1960

**Edwin "Buzz" Aldrin on
the moon, 1969**

Men took their first steps
on the moon in 1969.
Here Buzz Aldrin poses
for a photo taken by his
fellow astronaut, Neil
Armstrong. Aldrin wears
an air-tight space suit with
a tank that provides
oxygen. Without this
equipment, he wouldn't
have been able to breath!

Quiz:
Look closely at the
photo of Buzz Aldrin.
What can you see
reflected in his helmet?

Places to visit:
Here's another reason
to visit the Smithsonian
National Air and Space
Museum in Washington,
D.C. … you can learn
more about space flight!
The Apollo 11 command
module Columbia, which
carried Neil Armstrong
and his fellow astronauts
to the moon, is on display.

Man on the Moon ...

Buzz Aldrin and Neil Amstrong explore a vast new world.

Have you ever gazed at the moon and wondered what was up there? In ancient times, some thought the moon was a god that controlled their lives. People gradually began to learn more about the moon. About 400 years ago, scientists called astronomers* used the first telescopes* to look closely at the moon's surface. They found that this surface was rough and full of craters and other rocky formations. The more people learned about the moon, the more some of them wanted to travel there.

Then in 1959, the Soviet Union* sent an artificial satellite* up to the moon. This amazing machine, called Luna 3, landed on the moon's surface and took the first up-close pictures ever seen. People around the world were amazed at the images, and they decided it was time for humans to visit the moon themselves. Ten years later, United States astronauts* on the space flight Apollo 11 finally achieved this goal.

On July 21, 1969, astronauts Neil Armstrong and Edwin "Buzz" Aldrin became the first people to walk on the moon. Photographs of Armstrong and Aldrin showed them as lonely figures on a vast, rocky landscape in the blackness of space. Other images showed the Earth from the astronauts' perspective, a planet looking just as small and fragile as the astronauts themselves. These images made people proud of the achievements of human exploration. But they also reminded people of the importance of taking care of our planet, and avoiding things like pollution and war.

Photographer:
Neil Armstrong
Subject:
Edwin Aldrin walking on the moon
Date:
July 21, 1969
Place:
The moon

Picture of the Earth from space, 1972

In this photo the South Polar ice cap can be seen for the first time. Clouds float above the blue oceans and across the African continent. Can you see the island south-east of Africa? That is Madagascar.

1939–1945 Second World War

1961 Diana Spencer is born

1953 Elizabeth II becomes queen of the United Kingdom
1948 The Olympic Games are held in London
1948 Prince Charles is born

1910 1915 1920 1925 1930 1935 1940 1945 1950 1955 1960 196

Photoprapher:
Anwar Hussein
Date:
July 29, 1981
Place:
Buckingham Palace
in London, England
Subject:
Prince Charles and
Princess Diana kiss
on a balcony of
Buckingham Palace
shortly after their
marriage

Good to know:
In 2005 Prince Charles
remarried. His wedding
to Camilla Parker Bowles
was overshadowed by
the death of Pope John
Paul II. The ceremony was
thus postponed from
April 8 to April 9.

"Wedding of the Century"

Prince Charles and Princess Diana hold the
"wedding of the century."

Lady Diana Spencer was no ordinary bride. She was about to marry
Prince Charles, the son of Britain's Queen Elizabeth II. Diana was going
to become a princess … and she had only just turned 20 years old.

Diana was glad her wedding day had finally arrived. Ever since she had
started her courtship with Charles, she had had no peace. News reporters
were always running up to her on the street and asking her questions.
Diana could hardly walk to the grocery store without attracting attention!

But today was her wedding day: July 29, 1981. Dressed in her lovely
bridal gown, Diana rode through the city of London to St. Paul's Cathedral,
where she and Charles would marry. More than a million people lined the
city streets as her carriage passed, all hoping to get a tiny glimpse of
the famous bride. When she processed into St. Paul's cathedral with her
father, 750 million people watched her on television … more people
than had ever watched an event on television before!

Pictures from Charles and Diana's wedding became instantly famous.
The royal couple seemed to have the perfect marriage. People in Britain
especially liked Diana, and she became one of the most photographed
British princesses … the people's princess.

Sadly, however, Charles and Diana were never completely happy as husband and wife, and their marriage didn't last forever. The couple divorced
in 1996. Then in the following year, Diana tragically died in a car crash.

1981 Wedding of Charles and Diana
1990 South African leader Nelson Mandela is released from prison
1996 Charles and Diana divorce
1997 Diana is killed in a car crash

1970   1975   1980   1985   1990   1995   2000   2005   2010   2015   2020   2025

Diana's life had ended sadly. But the photographs of her wedding day—and the happiness that they represent—are how most people in Britain like to remember their beautiful princess.

Newlyweds Prince Charles and Princess Diana kiss, 1981

These two are truly a royal couple. Diana's flowing dress and veil contrast with Charles' stiff uniform and medals. Romantic photos like this one gave people hope that Charles and Diana would be happy as husband and wife.

1939–1945 Second World War
1929–1941 The Great Depression
1945–1991 The Cold War

1933 Adolf Hitler becomes the head of Germany's government

1949 Germany is separated into two nations:
East Germany and West Germany

1961 The Berlin Wall is built

1910   1915   1920   1925   1930   1935   1940   1945   1950   1955   1960   196

Photographers:
Ingo Röhrbein (p. 29)
and Andreas Springer
(p. 30)
Subject:
The fall of the
Berlin Wall
Date:
November 10, 1989
Place:
The Berlin Wall in
Berlin, Germany

**Soviet army in Berlin,
1945**

Soviet troops raise their
country's flag over a
conquered and ruined
Berlin. Germany had lost
World War II, and Berlin's
weary citizens would
soon live in a divided city.

A Nation United

The people of Berlin tear down a hated wall.

The city of West Berlin had become an island … an island that lay right in the middle of a foreign country! West Berlin was part of Berlin, a city that had once been the capital of Germany. But by 1949, war had divided Germany into two countries: East Germany and West Germany. Berlin now lay in the center of East Germany, but not all of Berlin belonged to that country. Little West Berlin was part of West Germany.

Leaders in West Germany and East Germany didn't agree on many things. East German leaders believed in a type of government called

Communism,* and they were allies of the Soviet Union.* West Germany was an ally of the United States, the Soviet Union's main rival. Yet many East Germans—especially those in East Berlin—didn't like living in their own country. They were watched closely by others who lived around them. If they said or did something wrong, they could be reported to the government and even imprisoned. People in West Berlin, however, were freer to do and think what they wanted.

So East Berliners began moving to West Berlin. Soon East German leaders feared that too many people would leave their country forever. So in 1961, they decided to build a big wall that further separated the island of West Berlin from East Berlin. This wall—the Berlin Wall—prevented East Berliners from traveling to the West.

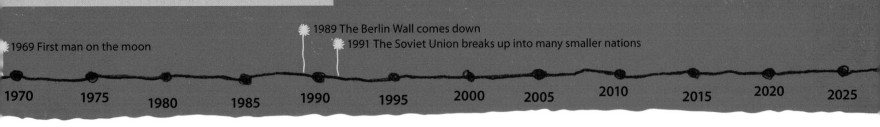

Fall of the Berlin Wall at the Brandenburg Gate, 1989

It's time to celebrate! East and West Berliners are reunited at the Berlin Wall, which would soon be torn down piece by piece. Behind the wall you can see the famous Brandenburg Gate, with its beautiful columns. Soon it would become a symbol* of a unified Germany.

The Berlin Wall divided people in many ways. It separated families, friends, and neighbors from each other. As time went on, life for East Berliners became much harder than it was for West Berliners. And if East Berliners tried to cross the wall in secret, they could be shot and killed by armed guards in watch towers!

But people cannot remain divided forever. As time went on, the East German government gradually lost power. At last, on November 9, 1989, the people of East Berlin were allowed to visit West Berlin. Thousands flooded across the wall, and cheers were heard around the city.

Soon, people throughout the world saw pictures of West and East Berliners sitting together on top of the wall. These pictures helped unite West and East Berlin into one city, and they helped make Berlin the capital of a united Germany. Eventually, other European countries gave up their Communist governments. Even the Soviet Union—the world's leading Communist nation—split up into many countries. The world that created the Berlin Wall had forever changed.

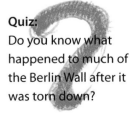

Quiz:
Do you know what happened to much of the Berlin Wall after it was torn down?

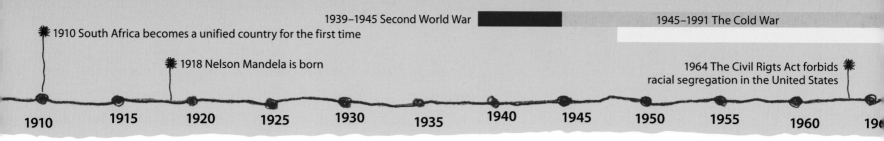

Photographer:
Greg English
Subject:
Nelson Mandela
and his wife Winnie
salute the crowd after
Nelson is released
from Victor Verster
Prison.
Date:
February 11, 1990
Place:
Cape Town,
South Africa

Image of Freedom ...

A South African hero is returned to his people.

Nelson Mandela came from a royal family. His great-grandfather had been
a king of the Thembu people, and his father was a village chief.* Nelson
was destined to become a great leader himself.

But when Mandela was born, his homeland was part of a country called
South Africa. The country was ruled by white-skinned people who
mostly spoke English, while Nelson's people were dark-skinned and spoke
a language called Xhosa. So young Mandela's family sent him to a school
where he could learn to read and write in English … and to become
an important man throughout his homeland.

South Africa was changing, and Nelson's people were finding life harder
and harder. In 1948, the new South African government began the policy
of apartheid,* passing laws that separated black and white South Africans.
In apartheid, whites went to the best schools and got the best jobs. Most
black South Africans could only toil in mines or do other dangerous or
low-paying work. Blacks were not allowed to live among whites. They could
not even travel to certain places in their own country.

Nelson wanted to make the lives of his people better. He joined the
African National Congress (ANC), a group that fought against apartheid.
Soon the South African government became fearful of Nelson and
the ANC, and Mandela was arrested in 1962. Nelson would spend twenty-
seven years in prison.

But Mandela did not remain quiet in his jail cell. He wrote letters to his
friends on the outside … and to leaders in other countries. Over time,
Mandela became his nation's most famous anti-apartheid leader.

32

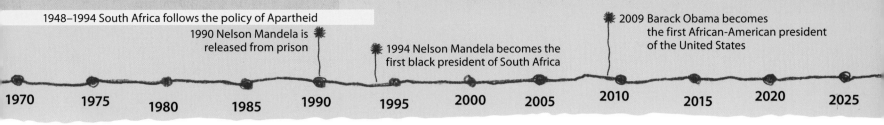

1948–1994 South Africa follows the policy of Apartheid

1990 Nelson Mandela is released from prison

1994 Nelson Mandela becomes the first black president of South Africa

2009 Barack Obama becomes the first African-American president of the United States

1970   1975   1980   1985   1990   1995   2000   2005   2010   2015   2020   2025

Nelson Mandela released from prison, 1990

Even though he spent many years in prison, Nelson Mandela never gave up on his dream of a South Africa without apartheid. When he was finally released in 1990, photos showed Nelson and his wife Winnie saluting the crowd with raised fists. These images symbolized* the power of a new South Africa.

More and more governments around the world began criticizing apartheid. Foreign businesses decided not to work in South Africa, and the country's economy became weak. In 1990, the government decided it would begin ending the apartheid system. It also decided to release Nelson Mandela from prison.

On the day Nelson got his freedom, photographers captured the image of Mandela and wife Winnie triumphantly returning to their people. Nelson Mandela, the son of a village chief, would soon become his country's first black president.

Good to know:
Even when Nelson Mandela was a baby, his parents knew he would inspire change in his country. They gave him the Xhosa name Rolihlahla, which can mean "trouble maker" in English!

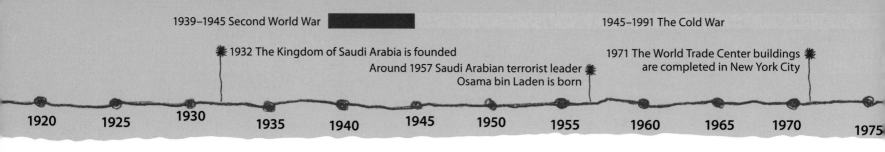

1939–1945 Second World War

1945–1991 The Cold War

✳ 1932 The Kingdom of Saudi Arabia is founded

Around 1957 Saudi Arabian terrorist leader ✳
Osama bin Laden is born

1971 The World Trade Center buildings ✳
are completed in New York City

| 1920 | 1925 | 1930 | 1935 | 1940 | 1945 | 1950 | 1955 | 1960 | 1965 | 1970 | 1975 |

Photographer:
David Drapkin (p. 35)
and
Steve Winter (p. 36-37)
Subject:
Manhattan is covered
in smoke after the
World Trade Center is
attacked by terrorists
Date:
September 11, 2001
Place:
New York City

America Attacked ...

New York City suffers in a cloud of terror.

The morning of September 11, 2001 was a beautiful one in New York City. The sky was clear and bright, and the temperature still warm at the end of summer. New Yorkers were on their way to work—ready for another busy day in a big city.

Suddenly people looked up at the twin towers of the World Trade Center, New York's two tallest skyscrapers. The north tower had been hit by an airplane! At first, people weren't sure if it was a small plane or a large plane, and they didn't know who was responsible. Then, just as suddenly as the first plane hit, another airplane smashed into the top of the south tower. New York was being attacked! Reporters soon found out that both planes had been hijacked* by terrorists.* Hundreds of innocent passengers were on the planes, and all of them had been killed.

But the terrible events would not end there. The damage that the airplanes had done to the twin towers made them too weak to stand. As people watched in horror, the south tower collapsed to the ground in a cloud of smoke. Minutes later, the north tower did the same thing. Thousands of people were working in the twin towers on that day, and many of them would die in the collapses.

Even though New Yorkers were shocked at what was happening, some were able to take photographs of the horrible scene. Soon, people learned that the Pentagon Building* in Washington D.C. had also been attacked. The same terrorist group that destroyed the twin towers had also hit America's capital city!

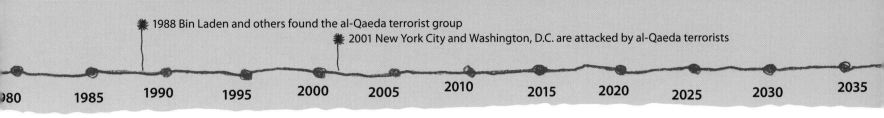

2003–2010 The Iraq War

✳ 1988 Bin Laden and others found the al-Qaeda terrorist group
✳ 2001 New York City and Washington, D.C. are attacked by al-Qaeda terrorists

980 | 1985 | 1990 | 1995 | 2000 | 2005 | 2010 | 2015 | 2020 | 2025 | 2030 | 2035

**Manhattan on
September 11, 2001**

Has New York City gone up in smoke? Terrifying images like this one showed why September 11, 2001 was one of the worst days in American history. Notice the Statue of Liberty at the left of the photo. Many Americans consider "Lady Liberty" to be a symbol* of American freedom and hope. But she looks small and lonely—almost sad—in this picture of chaos.

Images from 9/11 made people think about the United States in new ways. How could a small group of terrorists cause so much damage to America's most important cities? What could people do to prevent future attacks? In the coming months and years, many nations would pass laws making it harder for people to cause harm on airplanes. But the threat of future terrorist attacks remains to this day.

Quiz:
Before they were destroyed on September 11, 2001, the twin towers were New York City's tallest buildings. What is the city's tallest building today?

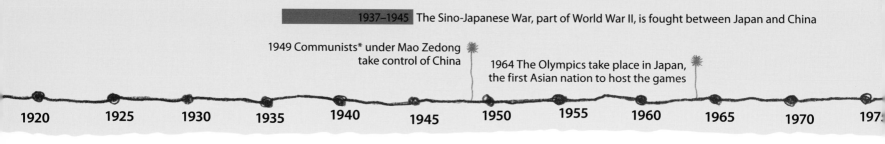

Photographer:
Clive Rose
Subject:
Fireworks explode over the Beijing National Stadium during the opening ceremonies for the 2008 Olympic Games
Date:
August 8, 2008
Place:
Beijing National Stadium in Beijing, China

Good to know:
China has more people than any other nation … more than 1.3 billion!

Chinese Celebration ...

A great nation holds a colorful Olympic Games.

The Chinese people have always loved fireworks. For centuries, these colorful explosives have lit up important Chinese festivals. So when China held its first Olympic Games* in 2008, fireworks covered the skies of Beijing—China's capital city—on the games' opening night.

The Chinese had undergone great changes before that night in 2008. For centuries, China had been an isolated nation … a nation that many outside countries found strange and mysterious. But beginning in the 1980s, more and more people from other places began living and working in China. Soon, Chinese leaders began creating powerful businesses that sold clothes, computers, televisions, and other products worldwide. Ordinary Chinese people moved from poor villages in the countryside to big cities where they could find good jobs. All of these changes made China seem less mysterious to the outside world.

Then in 2001, the Chinese got a chance to hold a party for the whole world, a party that could show how much China had changed. The city of Beijing was awarded the Olympic Games, the world's most important sporting event.

For the next seven years, Beijing worked hard to build a beautiful Olympic village. Workers constructed apartments for the athletes to live during the games, as well as good roads and trains for traveling to the games. They also built the Beijing National Stadium, where many of the Olympic events would be held. This grand building would be known as the "bird's nest," because its walls were made of huge metal beams that curved and twisted like the twigs of a nest.

Late 1970s Under leader Deng Xiaoping, China begins to make its economy more prosperous
1989 Bloody repression of the demogracy movement in Bejing
1991 The Cold War ends as the Soviet Union breaks up into many smaller nations
2001 The United States is attacked by terrorists on September 11
2008 China holds the Olympic Games for the first time

1980   1985   1990   1995   2000   2005   2010   2015   2020   2025   2030   2035

All of China's hard work paid off on August 8, 2008, when the Olympic Games' opening ceremonies took place in the bird's nest. This amazing event featured thousands of Chinese performers in beautiful costumes. Images of the event on television impressed millions of people worldwide. They showed that China was no longer an isolated country … it was now at the center of a new world.

Opening ceremonies for the 2008 Olympic Games in Beijing, 2008

Fireworks light up the "Bird's Nest" stadium at the Beijing Olympics; the stadium is reflected perfectly in the water below.

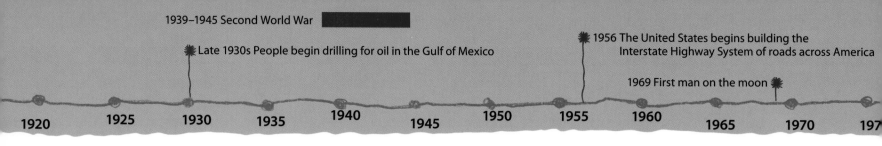

Photographer:
United States Coast Guard
Subject:
Coast Guard boats work to put out the fire at the Deepwater Horizon oil rig
Date:
April 21, 2010
Place:
Gulf of Mexico, near the coast of Lousiana, USA

Disaster in the Gulf ...

Oil gushes into the Gulf of Mexico—threatening plants, animals, and a way of life.

What would we do without oil? Most of us couldn't drive a car without gasoline, which is made from oil. Gasoline also fuels the airplanes that fly us to distant cities, as well as the trucks and trains that carry goods from one place to another. Oil is also used to make furniture, clothing, and many other things that we use every day. Because oil is such a necessary part of our lives, businesses that sell oil will travel almost anywhere to find it.

Many oil companies drill for oil in the Gulf of Mexico, a body of water that lies off the southeast coast of the United States. To get to the oil, companies use giant equipment called rigs to drill wells under the bottom of the sea. These wells can lie more than a mile (1.6 kilometers) beneath the water's surface!

In 2010, a terrible accident occurred at one of the gulf's oil rigs, called Deepwater Horizon. An explosion caused a fire in the building at the top of the rig. This explosion killed many workers, and the upper part of Deepwater Horizon sank into the gulf. The explosion also opened a big hole at the bottom of the gulf, where oil and harmful gases began shooting up into the water.

Television pictures of the gushing hole shocked people around the world. The hole needed to be "capped," or closed, before too much oil escaped. But closing the hole proved difficult, as it was so deep under water. Only after many months of hard work was the well finally capped.

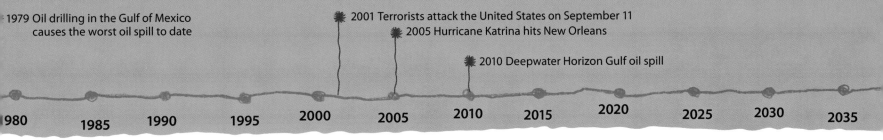

1979 Oil drilling in the Gulf of Mexico
causes the worst oil spill to date

2001 Terrorists attack the United States on September 11
2005 Hurricane Katrina hits New Orleans

2010 Deepwater Horizon Gulf oil spill

980   1985   1990   1995   2000   2005   2010   2015   2020   2025   2030   2035

Rescue boats at Deepwater Horizon, 2010

The brave rescue workers of the U.S. Coast Guard had a difficult job to do on April 21,
2010. A huge explosion had engulfed the Deepwater Horizon oil rig in flames and smoke.
Many people had died in the explosion, but the Coast Guard would save many other lives
and extinguish the fire.

Pelican covered with oil

Animals that have been covered in oil, like this pelican, have to be brought to rehabilitation centers by wildlife rescue workers. There they are cleaned, fed, and cared for, and finally set free again.

But during those months, the oil that escaped from the well caused great harm to gulf animals, plants and people. Photographers captured pools of oil floating in the gulf, as well as oil-covered birds and fish. People who fished for a living couldn't find work, as many sea animals had died or become sick. Eventually, the oil reached the shore, causing a horrible smell in New Orleans and other gulf cities. Some people even became ill because of the smell. The company that ran Deepwater Horizon had to pay billions of dollars to clean up the spill and provide money for the people hurt by the accident.

Pictures of oil-soaked animals helped people learn about the damage done by the gulf oil spill. Do you have a favorite animal that lives nearby? Maybe it's a colorful bird or a funny insect? Try bringing your camera to a park or woodland near your home. Then see if you can take a picture of an interesting creature. Be careful not to make too much noise when photographing an animal, or it might run or fly away!

Every day new images move the world, and history goes on.

Here is space for you to paste in pictures that you find moving or important.

Glossary

APARTHEID was a series of laws in South Africa that kept black and white people separate. Under apartheid, black South Africans were forced to live and work in poor—and often dangerous—places.

ARTIFICIAL SATELLITE is an object that people send into outer space. Once in space, artificial satellites orbit—or travel around—the Earth.

ASSASSIN is a person who kills another person, usually for money or as a kind of protest.

ASTRONAUT is a name used for a person trained to travel in outer space. This name is used for space travelers from the United States, the United Kingdom, and other Western countries.

ASTRONOMER is a scientist who studies planets, stars, and other objects in space.

ATOMIC BOMB is a kind of weapon that creates an explosion powerful enough to destroy an entire city. During World War II, the United States used atomic bombs to destroy the Japanese cities of Hiroshima and Nagasaki.

AVITAOR is a person who is skilled in flying airplanes.

CHIEF is a name for the leader of a group of people. Most chiefs control individual towns or villages, and they often come from families who have been chiefs for many generations.

CIVIL RIGHTS give people the freedom to choose how they live and work. Civil rights laws forbid governments from taking away people's freedoms.

COMMUNISM is a political philosophy, or way of thinking, that was supported by many governments in the 1900s. In Communist countries, such as the Soviet Union, most businesses and farms are controlled by the government. In Capitalist countries, such as the United States, most businesses are controlled by people outside the government. Few Communist nations exist today.

COSMONAUT is a name used for space travelers from Russia and the former Soviet Union.

ENGINEER is a person who helps make, maintain, and fix things by using ideas from mathematics and other kinds of science. Engineers who design buildings ensure that each part of the building is strong and stable, preventing the structure from falling down.

GLIDER is a "flying" machine that enables people to remain in the air without using an engine. Most gliders can only stay in the air for a short time.

HIJACKING is when a person takes over an airplane or other vehicle by force, often using guns or other weapons. Some hijackers, like those involved in the September 11 attacks, use airplanes to commit acts of terrorism.

HIMALAYA is a group of mountains in Asia. The highest of these mountains is Mount Everest.

ICE AXE is a tool used by people when climbing mountains. One end of an ice axe has a long, sharp piece attached to it. This piece can dig into ice and snow, helping a mountaineer climb up steep, icy slopes.

JAZZ is a kind of music and dance developed by African-Americans in the early 1900s. Jazz music is known, in part, for its complicated and exciting rhythms.

JET AIRPLANE is a plane that uses a jet engine to fly. Jet engines are powered by gasoline.

McCARTHYISM was a political movement in the United States. U.S. government leaders tried to identify Americans that they considered Communists, or supporters of the Soviet Union. The name McCarthyism comes from a U.S. politician named Joseph McCarthy, who was a leader of this movement.

MOP-TOP is a kind of haircut shaped like a bowl or mop. It became popular in the 1960s.

OLYMPIC GAMES are a huge event where athletes from around the world compete in different sports. One type of Olympics is held in the summertime, and it features running, swimming, and other warm-weather sports. The other type, held in the winter, features such cold-weather sports as skating and skiing. The word "Olympic" comes from the ancient Greek city of Olympia, where the first Olympic games were held more than 2,500 years ago!

PENTAGON BUILDING is the headquarters of the United States Department of Defense, which runs the country's military forces.

PUBLICITY PHOTO is a kind of photograph created to make a certain person, group, or thing more popular.

RACISM means hatred of an entire group of people, usually because of how they look. For example, white-skinned people who dislike all black-skinned people are racists. Racist laws are often created to take away the rights of people who look a certain way.

SEGREGATION exists when a particular group of people are separated from another group of people, often against their will. In the past, many laws in the United States, South Africa, and other countries forced black people to live separately from white people.

SOVIET UNION, or the Union of Soviet Socialist Republics, was a large nation that existed between 1922 and 1991. It was the world's most important Communist country. In 1991, the Soviet Union broke up into many smaller nations, including the country of Russia.

SYMBOL is something that reminds people of something else. The British flag, for example, reminds people of the United Kingdom.

TELESCOPE is a scientific instrument that uses special lenses to look closely at the night sky. Looking through a telescope lens, the stars and planets appear larger … and parts of the moon's surface can be seen more clearly.

TERRORISTS commit acts of violence, such as the killing of innocent people, to achieve certain goals. Many terrorist acts are committed against certain countries or governments.

Answer to the quiz questions:

Page 24:   Look closely and you can see an image of Neil Armstrong in Buzz Aldrin's visor. Armstrong was the astronaut who took this picture of Aldrin. You can also see the Apollo 11 spacecraft that the astronauts used to land on the moon.

Page 31:   Today remnants of the Berlin Wall can be found in many public places and museums. Parts of the wall have even been broken up into small pieces and sold as souvenirs.

Page 37:   Today, the tallest building in New York City is the Empire State Building … the same skyscraper that had been New York's tallest before the World Trade Center was built!

Library of Congress Control Number: 2011922845; British Library Cataloguing-in-Publication Data: a catalogue record for this book is available from the British Library; Deutsche Nationalbibliothek holds a record of this publication in the Deutsche Nationalbibliografie; detailed bibliographical data can be found under http://dnb.ddb.de

Picture credits:
AP: p. 33; Getty Images: p. 19, 21, 28, 35, 36–37, 39; Getty Images/Arthur Sasse/AFP: p. 12; Getty Images/Anwar Hussein: p. 27; Governor Bobby Jindal: p. 42; NASA: p. 24, 25; NASA/Smithsonian Institution: p. 7 below; Sue Ream: p. 31; RoyalGeographical Society: p. 15, 16–17; ullstein bild: p. 5, 22–23, 30; ullstein bild / Röhrbein: p. 29

Prestel Verlag, Munich
Prestel is a member of Verlagsgruppe Random House GmbH

www.prestel.de

Prestel books are available worldwide. Please contact your nearest bookseller or one of the above addresses for information concerning your local distributor.

Prestel Publishing Ltd.
4 Bloomsbury Place, London WC1A 2QA

Prestel Publishing
900 Broadway, Suite 603, New York, NY 10003

www.prestel.com

Editorial direction: Doris Kutschbach
Editing/copyediting: Cynthia Hall
Picture research: Andrea Jaroni
Design and Layout: Michael Schmölzl, agenten.und.freunde, Munich
Production: Nele Krüger
Art Direction: Cilly Klotz
Origination: Reproline Mediateam, Munich
Printing and Binding: Tlačiarne BB, spol. s r.o.

Verlagsgruppe Random House FSC-DEU-0100
The FSC-certified paper Hello Fat Matt 1,1 has been
supplied by Condat, Le Lardin Saint-Lazare, France.

ISBN 978-3-7913-7047-7